THE MINDFUL COLORING JOURNAL

THE MINDFUL COLORING JOURNAL

BRING POSITIVITY INTO YOUR LIFE

MIKE ANNESLEY

SIRIUS

FOR ANNA

Photos courtesy of Shutterstock.

SIRIUS

This edition published in 2022 by Sirius Publishing, a division of
Arcturus Publishing Limited,
26/27 Bickels Yard, 151–153 Bermondsey Street,
London SE1 3HA

ISBN: 978-1-3988-0958-1
AD007505UK

Printed in China

INTRODUCTION

The best instant fix for stress or anxiety is to push it aside by focusing your mind on something else. Mindful colouring is perfect for this. It's the easiest way to let the creative part of your mind take over from everyday preoccupations. In the process, you experience peaceful pleasure in productive activity. Each colouring project is a playground for your imagination. Your imaginative self and your worrying self are mutually exclusive, like sunshine and rain. Bringing colour into your moments and minutes will send your inner rain clouds packing. And the effect can be surprisingly long-lasting.

The pictures here offer an inspirational focus for creativity. In the accompanying text, you'll be prompted to think creatively about each particular subject and its implications for finding peace and fulfilment. You'll be prompted too to write down your thoughts – since self-expression can also be a route to self-healing.

The journal pages here offer you the freedom to chart your moods and reflections in whatever style you wish. You could jot down words and phrases or else do fully-fledged diary entries, or a mixture of both – it's entirely up to you. You could even add little sketches or mind maps if you like.

In addition, for each drawing to be coloured in, there's a dedicated space for you to engage in an illuminating dialogue with ideas prompted by the picture.

The beauty of colouring is your complete freedom to make the image as realistic or surreal by your choice of colours as your imagination wishes. It's a playground without rules.

And once you've completed an image, why not contemplate it and open your eyes and heart to its soothing or vitalising energies? Gaze at it mindfully, savouring its qualities in the moment. You are on the pathway of meditation: colouring is itself a meditative practice. Even your first steps offer a trustworthy promise of inner peace.

HOME SWEET HOME

How much does home matter to you? Do the stability and safety of your home, and the way you've shaped it to correspond with your needs and personality, ground your spirit and nourish your well-being? Or are you a restless soul, using home simply as a practical convenience – a base for your various adventures? Imagine yourself in your ideal home. How much would you have to change to make this a reality? What would its essential ingredients be?

Use the space below to remind yourself of what makes you happy in your home, in real life, as well as what you would ideally wish to change. Be imaginative in your adjustments: don't feel restricted by your actual circumstances.

_____

_____

_____

_____

_____

_____

_____

_____

Imagine leading your optimum lifestyle in this place. Who would you like to have as regular guests? How would you choose to entertain them? Which rooms would you spend most time in? What activities would you most enjoy? Think of how you could adopt these choices in your current surroundings.

Colour in the picture opposite while thinking about your perfect home in the perfect location. Think of the home's contents too as you work on the structure and surroundings.

Have patience with everything that remains unsolved in your heart... live in the question.

Rainer Maria Rilke

VOYAGE OF ADVENTURE

Think of the ocean, where the only visible changes are due to the weather, ocean currents and the passage of ships. Do you find the thought of the wild sea thrilling or daunting? If you were in the crew of a sailing ship, do you think you'd feel closer to nature? What other feelings would you have? Contemplate the sun's energy, powering all life and change. Winds couldn't blow anywhere without the sun to power them. Can you feel the vital force of the sun in your own life, filling you with positivity, even when the winds of change blow hard?

Use the space below to remind yourself of the direction of your life's voyage. Note what you hope to see and feel at your various destinations and the benefits you might acquire as you travel to get there.

_____

_____

_____

_____

_____

_____

_____

Imagine drawing upon the sun's energy and using it to propel yourself safely through life's ups and downs. Think of yourself as a mariner - you know the risks of any voyage but are happy to face them, with skill and wisdom, for the sake of incomparable rewards.

   Now, why not colour in the voyage opposite, as a reflection of your life's adventure? Remember, the winds of change are there to fill your sails, not to blow you off course.

FLYING LIKE A BIRD

Birds inspire us with their mastery of air, their lovely songs and their beautiful livery. What kind of bird do you find most attractive? Perhaps a majestic eagle soaring high above a valley, a charming little songster pouring its heart out from a bush, or a serene swan gliding across water? In this exercise, imagine what kind of bird you are or would like to be. Do you have bright plumage or soft, subtle markings that blend in with your surroundings? Are you a big, strong flyer or a nimble bird that loves to dart around? Which do you prefer: being part of a flock or foraging in your habitat alone or with a few companions?

Use the space below to list the qualities you admire in the bird of your thoughts – it might include, for example, wisdom, intelligence, proud self-confidence, reticence or a sweet voice raised in song.

_____

_____

_____

_____

_____

_____

_____

_____

Once you've listed the qualities you admire, close your eyes and focus on each quality at a time and then think how you can apply them all to your own life.

Now, why not colour in the picture opposite to remind you of all the grace and colour that birds can bring into our lives?

There are two ways to
get enough. One is to
continue to accumulate
more and more. The other
is to desire less.

G.K. Chesterton

_____

_____

_____

_____

_____

_____

_____

_____

_____

_____

_____

_____

_____

_____

_____

_____

_____

_____

_____

_____

_____

_____

_____

_____

_____

_____

_____

_____

_____

_____

_____

_____

PLAYTIME

How good are you at playing – like a child, or a cat having fun with a ball of wool? However seriously we take our responsibilities, play is a vital safety valve for our energies. What form does play take for you? Do you perhaps find it in carefree leisure time with your partner, friends or family? Does sport or some other physical activity (anything from gardening to wild swimming) help you discover well-being? Or is creativity – writing, painting, acting, music and so on – a more important source of inner refreshment for you? Could you bring more play into your life? If so, how would you go about it? What benefits would it bring? And how would you recruit others to join you in your playtime?

Write down some words below that capture the spirit of 'play' for you. They might include, for example, 'silliness', 'nature', 'imagination' - the choice is yours. Then consider where you find those values currently and where else you might look for them.

_____

_____

_____

_____

_____

_____

Treat the picture opposite, while you are colouring it in, as itself a form of play. Be free in your choice of colours - for the cat as well as the wool! Do you sense within yourself, while your image is forming, something like this playful kitten fascinated by new experiences?

WONDERS ABOVE

On a clear night, do you ever look up at the sky and admire the immensity of star fields or the pitted, sharp-edged moon? Do the heavens fill your heart with awe, however briefly you might hold them in your gaze? Do you find, at times, that focusing on infinity puts any troubles you have in a helpful and healing perspective? The night sky offers gifts of both wonder and consolation – so why not open yourself more often to these blessings from on high?

Note down here what you find most inspiring about space - perhaps the sheer immensity of this mysterious realm, or our human achievements in mapping and even visiting it, or possibly the beauty of planets such as Saturn with its rings? Try to think of half a dozen words that represent your feelings about these things.

_____

_____

_____

_____

_____

_____

_____

Reflect on the idea that the miracles of space are matched by the miracles of our own world, in nature and the human body and brain. Imagine too that somewhere out there may be astonishing phenomena – the fact that we'll never encounter them doesn't make them any less real.

Now, colour in the night view opposite, with moon and stars, partially veiled by clouds. Think of this as your personal memento of the wonders beyond our ken.

If the Milky Way were not within me, How should I have seen it or known it?

Kahlil Gibran

LEAP HIGH

Dolphins leap gracefully out of the ocean – it's an instinctive reflex of their being. Do you believe it's in our own nature as humans to be graceful in any way? Could it be, for example, that we show grace when we're selfless, or artistic, or conscientious, or compassionate? Do you know people whose lives are perfect expressions of their own intrinsic goodness? Perhaps such people dance to their own lovely tunes, without even having to think about it. What's the best melody you carry inside yourself and how often do you dance to it, with unselfconscious grace?

Imagine you're giving a solo dance performance that reflects all you value in yourself – adding up to your own blend of grace. List below the characteristics you'd need to convey. Then make a note of the people you'd like to join you onstage in duets and ensemble pieces. What qualities would you expect them to display?

_____

_____

_____

_____

_____

_____

_____

As you colour in the leaping dolphin opposite, dwell on the attributes that make you rise to your greatest heights. Think also of what you've done, are doing or plan to do that might qualify you as one of life's graceful dancers.

BONDED IN LOVE

Think about your most precious relationship, in a spirit of appreciation and gratitude. How much better are you together than alone? How do your different personalities complement each other? How much similarity is there among the inevitable differences? How do you safeguard each other? How has your life been changed by this soulmate? How, if at all, has your character been changed? Then ask yourself if you can do more to affirm and strengthen the love between you. Could you communicate more effectively? Could you be more tolerant? Could you look at situations more often from the other's viewpoint?

Write down here a simple five-point plan for making your relationship even more rewarding and empathic. Resolve to put that plan into practice.

_____

_____

_____

_____

_____

_____

_____

Consider how lucky you are to have been able to deepen your life through having such a special person to share it with.

Colour in the pair of swans opposite, as a symbol of the love you feel for your partner, or your ideal partner if you haven't met them yet. Use colours to show the strength of your feelings – swans may be white on the outside but their inner world is vivid and dynamic.

GREEN FINGERS

Our best qualities are often those we need to nurture within ourselves, like someone growing and maintaining a garden. Patience, for example, takes a considerable input of work. So do tolerance, forgiveness, courage and many other qualities we treasure. Even love, of the most settled and satisfying kind, flourishes best when you put your best efforts into it. What are your optimum qualities and what have you been doing to ensure they're available to you when you need them? What have you learned about yourself while attempting to grow such values and gifts in your inner garden? Do you foresee, in times ahead, a wonderful flowering? How can you prepare the ground to make it fertile for your self-development?

Briefly describe the highlights of your garden of inner qualities, as if you were showing them to a visitor. What pleases you most of all? What has required you to work hardest for a result that makes you proud? What plans do you have for future growth? What changes will you make?

_____

_____

_____

_____

_____

_____

_____

Colour in the picture opposite as an expression of the work you're doing to ensure your best qualities flower abundantly in the light of day, whatever the weather.

SPIRAL OF LIFE

Spirals suggest movement, dynamism, progression. In the drawing here they are used, within a circle, as the basis of a mandala – a symmetrical image on which to meditate, with a view to attaining inner peace. You may be surprised that geometry can offer a key to relaxation, but think about it: the beauty of a pattern is its detachment from our anxieties and desires. Have you tried meditation before? Just drawing or colouring in a mandala is a meditation in itself. The next step might be to spend time focusing mindfully (with relaxed concentration, staying as much as possible within the moment) on any of your coloured artworks and letting their healing energy lightly enter your mind.

First, try meditating on the spiral mandala before you colour it in. Spend a few minutes relaxing and letting your gaze wander around the image, absorbing all its features. After you've finished, write down below some of the thoughts that crossed your mind – however irrelevant. Don't judge yourself for not being more relaxed: the point is to let go of self-judgement.

_____

_____

_____

_____

_____

_____

Colour in the mandala. Then, whenever you feel like it, try the meditation again. Think of yourself as looking into the mirror of your own creativity and finding peace there.

Life is a balance of holding on and letting go.

Rumi

HORSE POWER

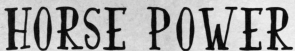

When you look at a horse, what do you see? The answer to that question will depend on the creature's breed, colour, age and condition, but imagine you see one that's youthful, strong and sleek, at play in a paddock. Do you sense – and perhaps even envy – its agility and power, its capacity for speed? Do you detect, in its facial features and demeanour, its history of close alliance with humankind? Horses are both free and compliant – think about this contradiction for a moment. When you ponder on a horse moving at speed, do you think of it galloping alone, a denizen of the wilderness, or do you wish you were its rider, thrilled by its boundless energy? In your imaginary horse ride, are you in control and happy to leave your pace and direction to your steed? Which would you prefer: trotting or galloping?

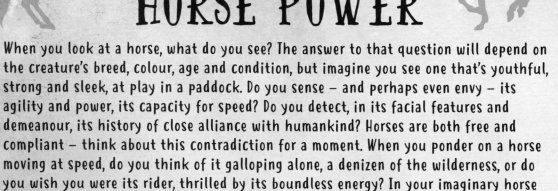

Imagine a horse you've encountered is admired as a fount of profound animal wisdom. Write down here some deep truths it might convey to you, about life in general and your life in particular.

_____

_____

_____

_____

_____

_____

_____

Contemplate the beauty and power of horses – and their incredible dignity. Imagine yourself bringing these and other qualities to life as you mindfully colour in the horse opposite.

MUSHROOM MAGIC

On a country walk all you have to do sometimes is look down to see miraculous nature. How often do you tilt your gaze downwards? Do you really engage with what's there – not only, say, the mushrooms or ferns, or whatever you might find, but also the insect life on and around them? Do you ever get down on your knees for a closer look? Do you ever take a magnifying glass with you on your walks, for larger-than-life inspections? Mushrooms are a reminder of what we so often overlook, even though it's right there under our noses. Their colours and textures, though subtle, can be incredibly beautiful. Why not make a resolution to appreciate nature's more refined pleasures, as well as its obvious highlights such as birds of prey and colourful flowers? Don't miss the understated.

See if you can think of some underrated natural phenomena – commonplace and small-scale but worthy of anyone's admiration. Write down your candidates below, based on lifelong experience.

_____

_____

_____

_____

_____

_____

Now, colour in the mushrooms opposite – and the little creatures that lurk among them. As you do so, imagine getting really close to nature's secret and subtle beauties.

TEEMING SEA

Where does your gaze tend to rest when you're walking an ocean shoreline – far out to sea or down into rock pools? The sheer abundance of life in a rock pool is amazing – all the more so because it thrives in seawater, an element so different from the air we breathe. A rock pool is a miniature world. It presents a selection of nature in which we can immerse ourselves imaginatively. Yet it gives us a taste of something grander, more sublime: the unimaginable fecundity of life on the ocean floor. It's unlikely you'll know the names of most creatures you see in a rock pool, but that by no means detracts from their impact. In your imaginary encounter, savour the variety of shell shapes and textures, and the hidden life forms they conceal. And what could be more strangely exotic than the starfish or seahorse? The deep holds unfathomable wonders.

What do you most enjoy experiencing when you visit a beach? What are the strangest life forms in the sea? Make a list of the weirdest phenomena you can think of.

_____

_____

_____

_____

_____

_____

_____

Why not colour in the glimpse of deep-sea life, opposite? Imagine yourself discovering unknown shellfish for the first time, startling in their vivid hues.

YOUR FIREBIRD

The firebird, or phoenix, once thought to be reborn from its own ashes, is a creature of myth, not real life. Why not adopt the bird as your 'spirit companion' and equip it with superpowers to make your life more peaceful or fulfilled? With such a miraculous ally, how would you use its talents? Would you recruit it to help you overcome your hardest challenges? If so, how in particular would you task it to assist you? Or would you summon your firebird as part of your toolkit for aspiration? It might give you a lift in your career, for example, or offer you the edge in sporting or artistic endeavours. Invoking an imaginary all-powerful companion like this is a technique often used by mind-body-spirit healers. It can really make a difference!

Write down in the space below a to-do list for your firebird helper to tackle, in order of priority. Feel free to put down small individual tasks as well as big life issues.

Colour in the firebird, either showing it emerging from the flames or giving it a multicoloured tail appropriate to a creature of your imagination. Once you've completed your image, meditate on it, taking its creative energy into your heart.

HIDDEN TREASURES

Sometimes the most precious things in life are right there under your nose, unobserved until you make an effort to look for them. Among the oak leaves in this image are acorns – which you'd expect. But how long does it take you to notice the butterflies and berries? Being mindful means, among other qualities, being alert to what you might previously have overlooked. Do you fully appreciate your friends, and all they do and say to show they care about you? Do you value the nature that can be found all around you, even if you live in a city? Are you aware of the workers who bring your mail, clean your streets, keep your power connected, and supply you with food and other necessities? Colour in this natural scene in a spirit of gratitude for life's everyday blessings.

Use the space below to make a gratitude list. Itemise the things you might at times have taken for granted – the small treasures that are all too easily overlooked.

_____

_____

_____

_____

_____

_____

Now, why not colour the woodland cameo opposite in a spirit of gratitude for life's countless blessings? Make the butterflies and berries sing with colour to acknowledge your appreciation of their value to the mindful soul.

Nothing external to you has any power over you.

Ralph Waldo Emerson

JOURNEY OF THE HEART

What could be more romantic or exciting than a hot-air balloon ride with someone you love? Drifting high above everyday stresses, you'd share the wonder of far-sightedness – a clear view for a hundred miles. What exactly would you hope to see? The places that mean most to each of you – where perhaps you first met or went on holiday together? (As this is an imaginary ride, you can ignore geographical realism.) A world healed by your love, where war and suffering are unknown? A future that has solved the problem of climate change through global cooperation and breakthroughs in science? Take a journey of the heart through your vision of the kind of world you dream of inhabiting. Look down on an earthly paradise.

Use the space below to devise a mission statement for the new world you'd love to see below you. What values would everyone hold dear? What priorities would all world leaders follow? What would be plentiful to all inhabitants?

_____

_____

_____

_____

_____

_____

Now, colour in the image, in a spirit of hope for the future – of your relationship, and of planet Earth.

All true artists, whether
they know it or not, create
from a place of no-mind,
from inner stillness.

Eckhart Tolle

PATIENT KINGFISHER

A kingfisher, perched patiently above water, suddenly dives to catch a fish in its bill. Sudden, decisive action like this is often the best course in our own lives. Do you sometimes spend ages weighing the pros and cons of a dilemma? If so, do you lack confidence in your own judgement? Or are you a perfectionist, wanting to master all the facts before taking action? Why not imitate the kingfisher? Wait patiently when you need to, then move, with conviction, at the right moment – don't miss your goal by diving too early or too late. The kingfisher knows when to try. Sometimes it might miss its prey – but isn't that too a life lesson we should learn? To sum up: don't miss the fish through thinking you might never catch it!

Think of a decision you have to make. List the pros and cons. Weigh both sides, then note down what action you might choose if you could muster kingfisher-like decisiveness.

_____

_____

_____

_____

_____

_____

_____

Why not colour in the kingfisher, waiting and watching? As you fill in its plumage, think of yourself being patient like the bird. What will you gain for your patience? (Choose any colours you like: there are many species of kingfisher in the world, all different.)

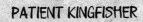

LOVELY LOTUS

The lotus flower is a symbol of peace, favoured in the East as a focus for meditation. The lotus grows out of mud – reflecting our own spiritual flowering out of our imperfect mortal bodies. But you needn't engage with philosophical ideas like this to benefit from meditating on a lotus mandala. If you're a complete newcomer to meditation, bear in mind that it's basically a simple practical tool for attaining inner peace. Do you feel you'd be useless at meditation, maybe because you can't empty your mind, or you're sceptical about its benefits, or you're a down-to-earth person with no spiritual talents? Put such thoughts aside: meditation is for everyone. Just do it. Rest your relaxed gaze on this lotus once you've coloured in the image. Don't judge any aspect of your resulting experience. Let the peace of pure imagery work on your mind.

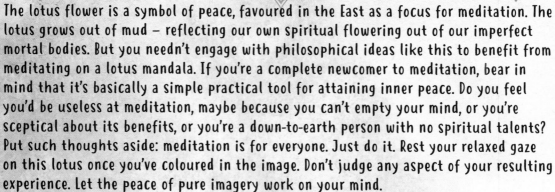

Before you start colouring, meditate on the lotus drawing for about 5 minutes and afterwards jot down below some of the random thoughts that no doubt entered your head while doing so. Then read your notes in a spirit of pure curiosity and self-learning – all meditators have random thoughts like this.

_____

_____

_____

_____

_____

_____

_____

Colour in the lotus mandala, adding your personal input to its timeless serenity.

It is in your power to withdraw
yourself whenever you desire.
Perfect tranquillity within consists
in the good ordering of the mind,
the realm over which you rule.

Marcus Aurelius

YOUR IDEAL CITY

Imagine you could bring into being your own city as a vacation spot for a long weekend. What features would your ideal city contain? Are you interested in history? Every building would tell its own fascinating story, with statues, plaques and visitor trails in the streets and squares. Do you have a special interest? There'd be a whole museum devoted to the subject. Does shopping press your buttons? The city could have unrivalled shopping streets — with bargain prices! Love theatre, music, cinema? There'd be an amazing range of shows, concerts and films to choose from every day of the week. Is gastronomy one of your pastimes? You could feast here on the finest cuisines of the world. Let your imagination make the journey — no airports, no lost luggage! Wander at will in the city of your dreams.

Make notes in the space below on what you'd do on your first day in your imaginary city. Describe the experiences you'd enjoy.

_____

_____

_____

_____

_____

_____

Now, why not colour in this ideal vacation haunt? Is it an island, or sited in a farmed landscape? That's your choice. As you work on your colouring, imagine the warm, friendly people you might meet here.

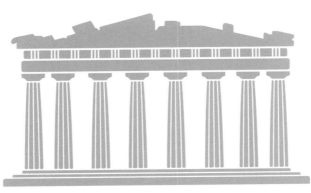

STAIRWAY TO HEAVEN

Some folktales and children's stories feature a plant that rises all the way to heaven. Would you dare to climb it? Would your hopes of heavenly reward overcome your fears? We all have different attitudes to risk, but sometimes enticing opportunities come our way, and saying no might seem cowardly. In this situation, would peer pressure play a part in your decision? Who in your life would urge you to be adventurous? Who would counsel caution? What would your own feelings be? What precautions would you take before your climb? Would you be anxious or excited as you took your first steps – or a mixture of the two? Remember that risk is a vital part of life – without it you'd be stuck in a rut. With every new attempt at success you risk disappointment, at the very least. However, learning to vanquish fear of failure is a basic life lesson.

In the space below, list some high-risk projects you'd like to consider embarking on some day. Think about both the risks and the advantages.

_____

_____

_____

_____

_____

_____

_____

Why not colour in the magic route to Paradise outlined in this drawing? As you do so, imagine yourself drawing upon your inner strength to take positive steps towards your goals.

FINDING THE UNICORN

Sometimes what we most desire seems as elusive as the mythical unicorn – not only was this beast incredibly rare, it was also shy and unapproachable. If you feel this way about one of your cherished hopes, could the idea that this hope is an impossible dream be itself a myth? After all, sometimes we spin negative myths around our lives, to give ourselves an excuse to remain in our comfort zone. Could it be that the unicorn isn't rare at all, just seldom sought? And could it seem shy only because you haven't yet approached it in the right way? Could there, in fact, be a unicorn that's looking for you but hasn't yet deemed the moment ripe to reveal itself? Why not abandon your preconceptions and go out to meet this creature with a warm, open heart? Who knows, perhaps it will welcome your friendly overtures.

Make a shortlist of some of your most precious hopes and wishes in the space below. Alongside each scenario note the first step you'd need to take to make your vision likelier to come true.

_____

_____

_____

_____

_____

_____

_____

Colour the unicorn in with a spirit of hope and positivity – and in the faith that a positive attitude can make good things happen.

LOVING NURTURE

Are you moved when you see an animal parent caring for its young? Do you find it inspiring to see how the adult guards its offspring and tends to its needs? We all need help initially, and in humans that help is often continued into the offspring's adult years – think of the sacrifices many parents make for their adult children. In many families there's a network of love, joining siblings, for example, in a lifelong bond. Think about these connections of the heart. What value do you place upon them? How far would you take your sacrifice, if needed, for a family member? Would you give up big chunks of your time? How about your job? Or your freedom? Knowing you'd be there for them is sure to give your loved ones reassurance, even if they've no reason at the moment to call upon you.

Use the space below to summarise the responsibilities you feel towards your closest family. List also the ways in which each family member might offer to help you in stressful times.

_____

_____

_____

_____

_____

_____

_____

_____

Now, colour in the scene opposite of a parent bear with its cub. As you do so, feel loving energy motivating your choice and application of colours.

APPLE HARVEST

What do you think of when you imagine an apple? You might think of the famous computer company, though the apple's primary associations are the opposite of high tech. Handling and observing an apple, from all sides, and then slicing it up and eating it, is a basic exercise in mindfulness practice: you focus all your attention on the apple, in the present moment – and on nothing else. An apple may have associations with health and well-being, but it can hardly be regarded as a universal symbol of these qualities. Instead, it is wonderfully itself: a simple tasty fruit. This makes it an excellent subject for a meditation. It carries no baggage. Simply enjoy it as you might enjoy sunshine or swimming. Be thankful for life's simplest things.

Try listing, in the space below, all the characteristics you can think of that an apple can have, perceived by all the senses. You may be surprised to find that there are, for such a simple thing, so many possibilities.

Now, transform the apple in the picture opposite into a multicoloured image – as a recognition that even the simplest fruits of nature can each reveal their own unique personality, if closely scrutinised.

FLAWLESS MANDALA

Mandalas, used as a pictorial focus for meditation, can be any shape but their key characteristic tends to be symmetry. A concentric design is perfect, since it provides symmetry in all dimensions. Designs based on flowers, leaves or snowflakes qualify well, or instead they could be purely abstract. The basic idea is to take your mind away from everyday life's flaws and imbalances into an ideal realm of the mind where nothing is amiss. You can lose yourself in a pattern just as easily as you can lose yourself in a depicted scene. The repeated elements of the pattern are subtly soothing, like a gentle rhythm in music. Lose yourself in this mandala, in a relaxed way. Savour its healing perfection.

As you contemplate this mandala outline, imagine it as an abstract quality, like love or truth or wisdom. Its very perfection symbolises the purity of the human heart. Write down below the particular quality you've chosen and some practical ways you can adopt to bring this virtue to life in your dealings with others.

_____

_____

_____

_____

_____

_____

_____

_____

Now colour in the mandala, giving it vivid life in the here and now – just as the actions you've listed will make your chosen quality real and tangible.

Live calmly. When the time comes, flowers bloom by themselves.

FLAWLESS MANDALA

CACTUS GARDEN

Houseplants bring the healing power of nature into your home, and watching them grow and flower, at their own relaxed speed, offers quiet refreshment for the soul amid life's usual bustle. What kinds of plants would you choose for an imaginary indoor garden? You might favour lush palms to remind you of warmer climes or feathery ferns you can brush against your hand for a pleasant sensation. Or perhaps orchids for a touch of exotic colour? Many, however, are drawn to the strangeness and variety of cacti, like funny little sculptures by a modern abstract artist. What qualities do you associate with cacti? Perhaps their quirkiness? Or their ability to survive neglect? Or perhaps they remind you how even a seemingly unpromising desert can burst into bloom after rain?

A cactus needs little nourishment: it flourishes despite adverse conditions. In the space below, write down some of the ways you've overcome difficulties and blossomed despite other people's – and maybe even your own – expectations.

_____

_____

_____

_____

_____

_____

Colour in the cacti display opposite. As you do so, resolve to be resilient, self-sufficient and happy in your own skin - but maybe not as prickly as these cacti!

CACTUS GARDEN

FLEETING BEAUTY

Butterflies have an elusive loveliness – often they don't stay still long enough for you to appreciate them as you'd like! That's why seeing one, and getting the chance to inspect it at close quarters, is regarded as a stroke of luck. You might, if you're really fortunate, see a whole cloud of butterflies. How do such lucky sightings of nature make you feel? Do you experience gratitude for nature's variety and abundance? Or for the fact that you've been for some reason chosen, in the lottery of life, as the lucky recipient of a marvellous revelation? Can you go for a country walk and not be disappointed or frustrated when you don't see something like this? Being a nature lover teaches us patience. It also teaches us to look properly, with mindful awareness – instead of being blinkered by our own preoccupations and anxieties.

Note in the space below some of the creatures you've recently encountered in nature or in city parks. What were they doing when you saw them? Which of these glimpses gave you most pleasure? Why do you think that is?

_____

_____

_____

_____

_____

_____

_____

Now, colour in the butterfly picture, as your tribute to all that is delicate, beautiful and ingenious in the natural world.